Micro-world of Trinity and also the world of Sun, Moon and stars. Now I have come to rest on my eternal seat in between the two eye brows.

Visualize- The rays and vibrations of power, peace, purity, love and bliss are spreading through each and every cell of the body rejuvenating and re-charging them. Dwell in this "Experience" for some time.

Post Meditation Suggestions

Now give two auto suggestions to the mind-

1] Let me remain in this elevated powerful soul conscious state throughout the day while performing my tasks under any circumstances which may try to disturb this state of consciousness.

2] Next day, at 4am, Amrit –vela when I begin my meditation [yog with Supreme Soul] let me begin from this elevated state of consciousness so that with each day I shall become more powerful, peaceful, loveful, blissful and pure.

APPENDIX - II

Pranayam Motivated Defaecation

A recent survey has shown that 14% of all Indians including the young suffer from mild to severe constipation. Severe constipation is very common in senior age group or the patients in Geriatric O.P.D. Several have to take enema on regular basis. Some have an experience of taking out the faecal nuggets with fingers. Lack of exercise, Pizza Burger Cola diet and Non-vegetarian diet are some of the important contributing factors. Over use of Over The Counter [OTC] pills or purgatives weaken the walls of intestine. Shortly it results in weak peristalsis or propelling movement of the intestine.

Hydrotherapy prior to P.M.D. Programme-
Warning- Never strain while defecating if you wish to avoid piles or fissures. Everything in yogic practices is done with ease.

Prior hydrotherapy- It is necessary to hydrate oneself well one day prior to P.M.D. Drink a minimum of 15 to 20 glasses of water throughout the day. It is necessary to drink water even if one is not thirsty. This is because with advancing age, the reflex initiating the drinking process gets progressively weaker. **The test for**

adequate hydration is that the urine always remains clear like water. Henceforth make it a practice to drink plenty of water throughout your life.

Jal Dhauti is a yogic kriya if performed for one month ensures adequate hydration and effective purging out of accumulated toxins.

Take four to five glasses of water or more if you can, no sooner one gets up at 4am.[Amrit-vela]. Warm water with a pinch of salt is helpful initially. A session of Pranayam after Amrit-vela meditation should be followed by P.M.D. Isabgol at night may help but required only initially. Learning Shuddhi kriyas like Jal Dhauti and Pranayam called Agnisaar helps.

Relaxation of mind by meditation plays a significant role. Never sing – Tu atki hai kanha, main tadapata yanha. This creates a negative programming of your mind. Instead sing. ,"Chal akela chal akela, Tera maila peeche chchuta, tu chal akela. This shall be a positive programming of your mind for the task at hand.

Do not contaminate the elevated Satvik consciousness achieved by meditation by taking a newspaper or your problems to the toilet seat. Focus your attention on your colon. Here the single pointed focus achieved by meditation helps greatly. Visualize about a faecal bolus stuck up at the appendix side of the colon. Now breathing deeply [abdominal breathing] visualize that the bolus is gradually getting unstuck. Now it is moving forward with each progressive contraction of the colon. Agnisaar at this point of time helps. Visualize that the bolus is now travelling in the ascending colon. Now it has entered the Transverse colon. Its forward movement has now become quicker. Visualize that now the bolus has entered descending colon and speedily going to the end of the rectum. Now a final push and it is out of the body. Do not strain at this point of time as it may cause piles to form. Each process has to be done with ease without straining at any point. Immense relief and joy at this point of time is beyond words. In fact you shall also see the relief writ large on the faces of the people around you, especially in an elevator.

Within a month you shall be colon trained and defecation shall be as easy as taking a breath.

BK- Rajayoga restores the SNS Versus PNS balance [Sympathetic Nervous System and Parasympathetic Nervous System] which is usually disturbed in Diabetes. This is the common cause of constipation in Diabetics.

Disturbed Internal balance of ions, sugar and lipids also contribute to N.C.D.s like Head ache, Migraine, Acidity, High B.P., Diabetes and Heart attacks.

Gut Like Protein –I and II released from Gastro intestinal tract helps in controlling appetite in Diabetes.

Medical science behind each and every ancient yogic practice needs to be investigated by a systematic research in Medical Institutes. There is a paucity of this type of research because the Indians themselves have stopped believing in the ancient Indian spiritual wisdom. Whole of the world is engaged in yog while Indians are pursuing the lifestyle of Bhog and Rog.

18-02-2019

BK Dr. Dilip V. Kaundinya

POETICBLUEZ

TONYA MORGAN SMITH

ACKNOWLEDGEMENT

I would like to personally thank some of the people who inspired me to write and go public with my work. I have a very small support group but their strength is as tall as a mountain. My mom, Lady T (Tina Morgan) who molded me to understand and embrace the gift that I have for writing. My 3 children, Iesha Stacy, Destini Stacy, and Andra Smith Jr. Even though it's my job to lead them, they have no idea how much they actually lead me. They are my inspiration, my motivation, and my reason. My husband, Andra Smith who has always encouraged me to focus on writing my because writing is my passion. His support has made it possible for me to start this amazing journey in my life and I'm very thankful. To my sister Wanda Morgan for being a great big sister and for sharing her son Dajhaun Morgan with me as if he were my own. My dad John Morgan for believing in me. To my friends for encouraging me and patiently waiting for me to finally publish my book. For the ones who broke my heart because without you I wouldn't realize how poetry embraces my heart when I'm hurting, and I wouldn't know how to appreciate the wonderful husband that I have. To God for keeping me in his arms through the good times as well as the hurtful times. I am so excited and this is only the beginning.

TABLE OF CONTENTS

If I Were A Writer 2
Lies 3
The Truck 4
Measure Of My Pain 5
If You Need Me 6
Who Are You 7
Don't Blame Me 8
When I'm Not Enough 9
Will You? 10
Cupid 11
How Did You Get Here? 12
Never Got Over You 13
The Flood 14
Do You Even Know 15
Jump 16
What Is Compatibility 17
I Miss You 18
His Plan 19
Your Message 20
The Pieces 21
Believe In Yourself 22
I Thought 23
Gambler 24
My Friend 25
Precious Heart 26

Is It Over	27
A Friend Like You	28
Thinking Of You	29
Friends First	30
All I Want Is You	31
Bare With Me	32
Losing You	33
Seasons No Reason To Change	34
Gods Beauty	35
The Rainstorm	36
Losing Yourself	37
Don't Wait Until It's Too Late	38
Ball Is In Your Court	39
Find Yourself	40
All About You	41
Bad Timing	42
The Destination	43
What Do You Want	44
Wish I Had More	45
My Promise To You	46
Empty	47
For You I Would	48
Tick Tock	49
Because Of You	50
You Are Appreciated	51
A Poem For Daddy	52
I Only Want To Love You	53

Good While It Lasted	54
Because I Love You	55
The Final Exam	56
Love Freely	57
Let Go	58
I Don't Know How	59
Sometimes I Wish	60
Pain	61
The Key To Happiness	62
Best Friend	63
We Tried	64
Just Tell Me	65
Forgive Me Please	66
Don't Love Me	67
Hurts Less To Walk Away	68
Good-Bye	69
Accusations	70
Addiction	71
Always	72
Choose You	73
Living In The Past	74
Shattered Glass	75
Pieces To A Puzzle	76
Try Again	77
The Storm	78
A Plan	79
Who Am I?	80

Friends Lovers Strangers 81
Victim To Yourself 82
Court Of Love 83
Sunshine In The Storm 84
Distant Love 85
Sisters 86
Getting Impatient 87
Can We 88
Finding Hope 89
Love Is Real 90
Familiar Strangers 91
Maybe Next Lifetime 92
To The Fellas 93
Momma Used To Say 94
Momma Used To Say 95
Momma Used To Say 96
Momma Used To Say 97
Momma Used To Say 98
Momma Used To Say 99
Momma Used To Say 100
Momma Used To Say 101
Momma Used To Say 102
Momma Used To Say 103
Momma Used To Say 104
Momma Used To Say 105
Momma Used To Say 106
Momma Used To Say 107

Momma Used To Say 108
Momma Used To Say 109
Momma Used To Say 110

POETICBLUEZ

IF I WERE A WRITER

If I were to be a writer
My work would be one of a kind
I'd get out my paper and pencil
And the words would flow from my mind.

I'd write about different experiences
I'd write about how I feel
I'd write about a fantasy world
And make you think that it was real.

I'd write about something exciting
I'd write about something true
And whenever you read my writing
You'd think that it happened to you.

I would love to be a writer
My paper would be my best friend
I'd tell it everything that I feel in life
I'd write until the end.

LIES

A green pepper and a red pepper are still peppers.

A WHITE lie and a BLACK lie
are *still LIES*

THE TRUCK

You can't expect me not to be afraid that you're gonna hit me
with the truck
If every time I give you another chance;
YOU HIT ME WITH THE TRUCK.

MEASURE OF MY PAIN

My pain shouldn't be measured by your morals.

IF YOU NEED ME

I don't know your exact circumstance
But I know that something's not right
I just want you to know that I am here
To help you win this fight.

I know that this is a fragile time
You need a real true friend
Just know that if you let me
I will be there until the end.

If you need a friend to talk to
I will gladly lend my ear
If you need a friend to support you
Rest assure because I am here.

If you need a friend to cry with
I have plenty of tears to share
If you need a friend to laugh with
I have plenty of smiles to spare.

If you just need someone
To help pass time
Just look and I'll be around
I may not always lift you up
But I will never let you down.

WHO ARE YOU

Who are you and where did you come from
It's like you're a mystery man

Everything that he won't do
You're telling me that you can

You're always here to lift my spirits
Whenever I feel down

And you keep me from feeling lonely
When I need someone around.

Who are you and where did you come from?

DON'T BLAME ME

You say the choice is mine
To put us back together
You say this time you promise
That your love will be forever
You say that you won't hurt me
Like so many times before
But I'm afraid if I take you back
It will just be another war.

WHEN I'M NOT ENOUGH

How long will this excitement last?
What happens when it fades?
Right now, the sun is shining bright,
What happens when there's shade?

WILL YOU?

When the sun goes away
And the clouds turn to gray
The lightening starts to slay
And the trees start to sway
Will your love for me stand?

When the road gets rough
And life gets tough
When a kiss is not enough
When we call each other's bluff
Will you still want to hold my hand?

Will You?

CUPID

My body is calling your name
My heart is calling your love
It seems like you're feeling the same
This must be sent from above.

My mind is stuck on you
I can't shake off this obsession
I don't even know what to do
This love has a deep aggression.

I should have never looked into your eyes
Your look captured my soul
In that moment I got hypnotized
And my heart surrendered control.

My love for you is deep
I hope you never walk out of my life
My heart is for you to keep
I'll pay whatever the sacrifice.

Bottom line is that I love you
Every day it continues to grow
I'll place no one else above you
And I'm never letting you go.

HOW DID YOU GET HERE?

I was lost before you came around
I didn't know I was missing, until I was found
My spark for life was totally gone
I didn't even realize that my candle was blown.
But then came you, and you opened my eyes
Your tenderness took me by surprise
You removed the clouds that were dark and gray
You bought back the sunshine to my day
Something was missing but I didn't have a clue
Then I realized that that something was always you
With you I feel love that drowns my pain
I never want to know life without you again.

NEVER GOT OVER YOU

I imagine that you're wondering
If what I'm saying is really true
It's confusing because I belong to him
But I have fallen in love with you.

I did not see this coming
I thought what we once shared had gone away
But my feelings for you came rushing in
Like the rain on a cloudy day.

I thought I could offer my friendship
Because we both had some healing to do
But your voice was my calm in the storm
And suddenly all I wanted was you.

I tried to hide my feelings from you
But I think you felt my vibe
You broke down my walls with your gentle words
In a way that I can't describe.

So now I wonder where we go from here
I would change it if I knew how
My feelings for you have fallen too deep
It's too late to turn around now.

THE FLOOD

For those of you who tried to drown me with your negativity;

Thanks for watering my garden.

DO YOU EVEN KNOW

When you walk in the room
My heart flutters, I feel faint, melt like butter.
Do you even know your strong effect
My vibe for you, does it even reflect
My feelings, my desires
Do you even know you inspire
Your smile says you know
But your action has a different flow
But I can't walk away
Until I know for sure
This curiosity is hard to endure
So there's only one way
That this will ever grow
And that's by me simply asking….
Do you even know?

JUMP

Turn off your thoughts
Turn off your fear
And JUMP.

You'll be glad you did.

WHAT IS COMPATIBILITY

I catch myself complaining that you give me 60% and not 100%.

I finally realize that 60% is your 100%.

It's the max that you know how to give.

We weren't built on the same scale.

We're not compatible.

I MISS YOU

I think of you
Each passing day
And words are never
Enough to say
So I send you this poem
To let you know
That you're very special
And I miss you so.

HIS PLAN

God has a plan for you
And he has already worked it through
Just follow His will and follow His way
And you'll get what's just for you.

YOUR MESSAGE

In your silence I hear a message
Though it may sound very absurd
I hear everything that you're saying
Though you do not say a word.

In your actions I feel a message
Though you show you don't care too much
You act like you don't want me in your life
But yet you always keep in touch.

In your look I see a message
Though you can't stare into my eyes
You pretend that you don't love me
But it seems like a big disguise.

In your distance I sense a message
Though you constantly walk away
Your mind thinks that I'm out to hurt you
But your heart believes in what I say.

In your voice I hear a message
Though your promises you never keep
There's something in your voice that proves
That your love for me is deep.

In this poem, I send a message
Though it's obvious by the things you do
You have forced me to walk away
I gave the benefit of doubt; But now I'm through.

THE PIECES

Let's pick up the pieces to our love……

And throw them further apart!

BELIEVE IN YOURSELF

Look for your special star
High up in the sky
Never let it slip away
Nor let it pass you by.

Let it be your friend at heart
Whenever you feel alone
Let it be there to lift you up
When you feel that you can't go on.

When situations get you down
Don't let your head hang low
Don't feel bad about where you've been
Just focus on where you're trying to go.

Things will be better, Days will be brighter
And your dreams you will achieve
Just hold on tight as you search for your star
And in yourself you will believe.

I THOUGHT

I thought I really needed you
I'm glad you helped me see
You're not too hard to live without
You do not breathe for me.

I thought that you were kind and great
And then you let me know
That you're really not even worth a damn
I'm glad you decided to go.

I thought that I would live so sad
Because you're so many miles away
But look, it doesn't phase me
I'm full of smiles every day.

I thought that you were the one for me
You showed me that I was wrong
I thought you were my strength
But even without you, I'm still strong.

GAMBLER

Don't go calling me wishing
That you had not stepped
Out of my life
Now you're mad cause you helped
The next man have me
Now you're out of control
Because you can't handle the thought
Of my body and soul
Being touched by another
As he holds me tight
Whispering I'm your lover
In the middle of the night
You threw me away
You were not concerned
Of my tears and fears
As for you I yearned
You saw her flicker of light
And you followed with no shame
Now you're running back
Because she blew out the flame
You thought the grass was greener
And you could afford the cost
But the game is over baby
You gambled; and you lost.

MY FRIEND

You are a very unique person
I'm glad to be called your friend
What we have is very special
And I will be here until the end.

PRECIOUS HEART

I want to open up my heart to you
But it's the biggest fear that I ever had
I've been in this situation before
And the way it ended was sad.

The wound, it never had time to heal
I still hurt sometimes from the pain
It would kill me if you took a knife
And cut it open again.

I want so much to trust you
Your eyes tell me it's okay
But my heart tells me to be cautious
Just in case you go away.

I tried to leave my past behind
And enjoy a brand-new start
But I must be realistic
Only I will care for my heart.

You are everything I ever looked for
I found you after all this time
I just hope that we'll finally see the day
That I am yours; And you are mine.

IS IT OVER

I'm sorry to write and bother you
But I'm feeling so confused
You make me feel so loved
But my feelings feel abused.

I remember all the times
That you used to treat me like gold
But now it feels that you have changed
Is it because our relationship is getting old?

With all my heart I love you
And I'll continue to let you know
But if you feel that it's not me you want
Please tell me and I'll let go.

You are still a very sweet person
And I don't want us to end
But I used to feel like the sun in your shine
Now I barely feel like a friend.

A FRIEND LIKE YOU

Seems like yesterday we were strangers
Today we're the best of friends.
I could not find a better match
If I searched the world again.

There has always been a missing link
But you bring the chain together
The spot that was always empty
Is filled with you forever.

I know that we experience changes
Just like the seasons of the year
But what counts is whenever one of us are in need
The other is always here.

I promise to never leave you
I'll never take the friendship away
You're a very special person
I plan to enjoy you every day.

THINKING OF YOU

I thought I saw your face today
I reached and then it went away
I thought for a minute and then I knew
That I never cease to think of you.

FRIENDS FIRST

I know you don't believe me
When I say I'm into you
But if it's the last thing that I show you
You will see that it is true.

A man who can hold my attention
Is very hard to find.
But you are on my mind continuously
I feel you are one of a kind.

We've both been betrayed by love ones
So trust won't come with ease
But with Faith I'll take this chance
I'll unlock my heart and give you the keys.

I promise to never hurt you
Our foundation will stem from trust
Already we are one step ahead
Because above all, we were friends first.

ALL I WANT IS YOU

You asked me what I want from you
Well, let me break it down
I want to know if this is temporary
Or if you plan to be around.

It's true that we've been hurt before
But things happen for a reason
You were my sunshine after the rain
Let me help you weather your season.

You ask me what I want from you
I want you to believe in me
I see the beauty within your heart
That she chose to never see.

What was dull and unattractive to her
To me is a beautiful sight
To her what was just a dusty rock
To me is a jewel shining bright.

If only you would let me
I can be different from the rest
But I won't put forth all the effort
While you constantly give me less.

You ask me what I want from you
I hope this gave you a clue
I have no motive or intent to deceive
You see…. All I want is you!!

BARE WITH ME

How can I be so jealous
If I claim my love is real
Because I'm afraid you'll take advantage
Of the way I really feel.

How can I accuse you
When there are other women around
Because I'm afraid they will take the Blessing
That my heart has finally found.

How can I ever doubt you
If our love has a special touch
Because I've put so much into loving you
I can't imagine you loving me as much.

I beg you to be patient
For a change is on the way
I know that my jealousy is annoying
But I'll believe in love one day.

LOSING YOU

I wish there was an easier way
But what's done is done, what can I say
All I know is I love you so
And it tore me apart to let you go.

Just remember why we had to part
It was nothing like a change of heart
My feelings for you will always be true
I'll never get over losing you.

SEASONS NO REASON TO CHANGE

When you go through certain changes
It's like the seasons of the year
You think that you can't take it
And your mind fills up with fear.

Every time you think about it
You act a different way
You hurt the ones who love you most
And think that it's ok.

Your attitude changes completely around
You're not who you used to be.
You're not so easy to get along with
You're complicated to see

You turn down help when its offered to you
You turn down your only friend
You turn down a chance to be understood
And a chance to comprehend.

This madness is not called for
You don't have to act so strange
For complication is a part of life
But seasons no reason to change.

GODS BEAUTY

As I toss and turn
I cannot sleep
I glance out the window
And watch the cool air sweep
Those amazing features
In the middle of the night
As I watch by the stars' beautiful light
I see things that on one knows about
Like the flowers blooming
And the trees that sprout
Then suddenly the sun
Rises across the way
I'm a witness to Gods
Next beautiful day.

THE RAINSTORM

Like raindrops, my tears keep falling
This storm, will it ever cease
The more I realize that I love you
The more my pain will increase.

We both put forth the effort
But still our love won't fly
Will we ever find a solution
Or is it time to say good-bye?

Like a cloud, our times have darkened
When it rains, it surely pours
I only want to protect my heart
But to do so, I must let go of yours.

How can I let go of something so true
How can something so true hurt so bad
Love is supposed to mean happiness
But why are we left so sad?

Please somebody wake me up
I hope that I'm in a dream
Our love is falling like the rain in a storm
And is slowly floating down stream.

LOSING YOURSELF

When I look in the mirror
Who do I See?
A familiar face
But it isn't me.
The smile is different
It no longer lights the room
And the eyes no longer dance
Like the flowers that bloom.
The tears, though they're hidden
They are clear to see
And the strength is nothing
Like it used to be.
Her poise is crooked
She doesn't strive to achieve
She no longer fights her struggles
She doesn't even believe.
When I look in the mirror
Who do I see?
I don't know who she is
But it sure isn't me.

DON'T WAIT UNTIL IT'S TOO LATE

One day you'll see my love for you
One day you'll see that I was true
One day you'll hear the things I say
Let's hope it's not the day that I go away.

One day you'll remember what we had before
One day you'll wish you had given me more
One day you'll realize my willingness to stay
Let hope that's not the day that I go away.

BALL IS IN YOUR COURT

I say that I really love you
But you don't believe it's true
I try my best to prove it
By the things I say and do
You never even trusted me
Enough to say you love me too
But I can only tell you these things
Believing them is up to you.

FIND YOURSELF

I Know that you are struggling
To find out who you are
You're not impressed with what you've become
But to me you're a shining star.

I've tried to display what you mean to me
My heart lives for your touch
I've offered you all that I am
But I guess it's not enough.

To love you is to leave you
and give you all your space to grow
I hope my love helped water your seeds
As in your life you bud and sow.

I'm on a level that you are not
It's time I walk away
Perhaps our time just isn't now
But for you I will always Pray.

ALL ABOUT YOU

I should have never let my feelings go
Now I've fallen too deep
I've gotten so used to having you
Now I want you for keeps.

You're my day, my night, my sun and moon
You are my everything
I've felt a very special joy inside
Ever since I climbed upon your wing.

I hope we'll never lose this
It would tear my heart in two
You're the best thing that ever happened to me
My world is all about you.

BAD TIMING

You picked a fine time to tear me apart
In spite of my situation, I still gave you my heart
Even though I was hurting with a heart full of tears
And even through my brick wall that I built with my fears
You picked a fine time to tear me apart.

You picked a fine time to make my heart cry
You betrayed me and hurt me and you can't tell me why
When I tried to go forward you would knock me right back
When I'd follow your lead, you'd just kick me off track
You picked a fine time to make my heart cry.

You picked a fine time to make me hate me
After everything in life that I thought I could be
I feel ugly and worthless and have low self esteem
I have no desire to fulfill my hopes and dreams,
You pick a fine time to make me hate me.

THE DESTINATION

The destination means nothing
If you don't enjoy the trip along the way.

WHAT DO YOU WANT

You make a promise
Then break it
Give me your heart
Then take it
Protect me
Then stab me
Run me away
Then grab me
I'm confused
When you're tripping
You heal my heart
Then you rip it
I can't do this
It's too much
I'm torn down
Just too rough
This merry go round
Make it stop
We fall to the bottom
Then we're on top
1 minute you love me
Then you act like you don't
You'll be so kind
And then suddenly you won't
What is it with you
What did I do
This isn't necessary
Just say you're through.

WISH I HAD MORE

When we're mad at each other, you can't even imagine the hurt that I feel.
It's unreal
How my heart just explodes with pain
Like I'm getting stabbed over and over again.
As I cry
I ask myself why
Because I try
So hard to make this happen,
but it's like your heart keeps trapping
Your love inside and won't let it out.

If I could take you in my arms and hold you tight every night,
I'd chase away your fright
and maybe then you'll feel free to give your heart to me…
And all this fighting wouldn't be.
You see, I'm a lover not a fighter.
I feed from my desire.
My heart feels danger where there's anger.
I just want to love, not shed tears.
I can't take these spears that are coming at me.
I've spent too many years crying a river.
Now I feel real love and it makes me shiver with happiness.
But I also quiver from being sad because when I weigh the good with the bad;
The numbers don't add up to what I thought I had.

There's beauty in love, you have to see it, you have to want it,
you have to be it.
And the one thing that will always remain true,
is that I gave 100 percent to you.
I'm so sorry that it wasn't enough.
Wish I had more.

MY PROMISE TO YOU

Baby you mean the world to me
I hope you already know
Even though we have our differences
I will never let you go.

We both have nervous emotions
Afraid that the other will walk away
But baby you have my promise
That no matter what; I'll always stay.

I know it feels like we'll never be
But I'm working on it everyday
Sometimes you may not see it
But you'll have to believe in what I say.

I promise to make this happen
Soon it will be you and I
We love each other too much
To let this happiness pass us by.

EMPTY

You were broken
And you were low.
I promised to put you back together.
I gave so much of myself to you that now
You're full…
And I'm empty.

FOR YOU I WOULD

You asked me if I would cry for you
Truth is, I would nearly die for you.
I'd follow you to the moon and back
If that helps to keep our love on track.

You asked if my love is 100 percent
Baby in my life you were Heaven sent.
You worry that I will change my mind.
Why would I? You love is one of a kind.

I thought stars were only in the skies
But I see them every time I look in your eyes.
I can't force you to understand how I feel
But please always know that my love is real.

TICK TOCK

Time flies when you procrastinate.

BECAUSE OF YOU

For no reason, your feelings fade
I tried to trade it in for love
But it was hatefulness you were think of
You never said why, made me want to cry
But yet I still try.
Because it's too late for me not to care
Or to leave you and go anywhere
You see my love is real, it doesn't fluctuate
The way I feel will never be hate
But you set the tone
Like you wanna be left alone
So just remember that it was because of you
That I walked away feeling blue
Just remember that it was because of you
That I walked away.

YOU ARE APPRECIATED

I went to the store to buy you a card
And I was in there most of the day.
I think I must have read every card on the shelf
But none expressed what I wanted to say.

They described a great mother, sweet woman, and nurturer
Some described a unique woman of love
But none of them was enough to describe you
Because none combined all of the above.

When I say my Prayers at night, I thank him so much
For a woman of favor, so anointed and true
You have an overwhelming heart and I thank God for the opportunity
To love someone as great as you.

So if you feel you don't hear the words enough,
Please allow me to tell you today
That you are very special and you are appreciated
Much more that words can ever say.

A POEM FOR DADDY

My dad is very special to me
He is everything that a father could be
He understands if I make a mistake
And he always respects the decisions I make.

He stands by my side if I'm right or wrong
And his love and support helps make me strong
I'm glad that my dad is always here
To take away my doubt and fear.

In my life I hope he understands
That where ever I go
He'll always by my number one man.

I ONLY WANT TO LOVE YOU

I want our love to stay new
And never grow old
I want the candle to stay lit
And never grow cold.
I want to feel the butterflies
When I hear your voice
Baby I'll forever be grateful
That I am your choice.
I want the sound of my name
To bring a smile to your face
The moment you come home
I want to kiss and embrace
I want to always have something
To laugh about
We can do this baby; I have no doubt.
If we enjoy being happy
We won't have time to fight
If we appreciate each moment
Everything will be just right
I'll tell you each day how much you mean to me
Baby if we keep our minds positive
We can make this be.

GOOD WHILE IT LASTED

I tell you that I had a bad day
But you make it all about you
I promise to give you all my love
But you still don't believe it's true
I tell you I have a lot going on
And sometimes I just cry it out
But you make it seem like I changed my mind
And you fill your head with doubt.
We're too far gone to turn around
But not far enough to stay on track
It seems that I keep disappointing you
All I can do is give your love back.
So if you want to give up what we have
I will loosen up your chain
I will take the loss if it benefits you
But I will never love this way again.

BECAUSE I LOVE YOU

It's not that I'm tripping, I just feel like you're ripping
My heart right from my chest
I know that you love me, and will put on one above me
But sometimes my jealousy won't rest.
Sometimes I cry because I don't understand why
I'm afraid to love free and let go.
I know sometimes I spazz and really show my ass
I'm afraid of losing you though.
I don't give a dam, but with everything that I am
I plan to make you see
That as the days grow, ill figure out how to show
That you are the one for me.

THE FINAL EXAM

There's no need to study the course
If you're afraid to take the test.

Equip yourself, apply your knowledge
And trust yourself.

LOVE FREELY

Once your wings have developed
Let go and enjoy the flight.

LET GO

You have to learn to chill
Or you will burn everything you touch.

I DON'T KNOW HOW

If I tend to act very jealous
It's not to push you away
It's my way of fighting any temptation
That could cause your heart to stray.
I'm so busy fighting what's around us
That it seems like I'm fighting you too
I'm so busy hurting from broken a heart
That I'm afraid to trust in you
I see the frustration in your eyes
But I don't know how to let love flow
You want me to believe in you
But I don't know how to let my fears go.

SOMETIMES I WISH

Sometimes when the wind blows
I wish it would blow away my ability to love so deep.

Sometimes when it rains
I wish it would wash away my willingness to care so much.

Sometimes when the sun shines bright
I wish it would melt away my sensitivity

Sometimes when its thundering and lightening
I wish it would scare my tears away.

Sometimes when it's snowing
I wish I could be as cold as you.

PAIN

Sometimes holding on
Hurts worse than letting go

THE KEY TO HAPPINESS

Learn yourself

Spoil yourself

Love yourself

BEST FRIEND

Until we come this way again
Remember me as your dear friend
Remember that I love you so
Hold it close and don't let go.

Consider me a part of you
Share with me the things you do
Never feel that you're on your own
I got your back; You're never alone.

Contact me whenever you please
I will let you vent with ease
Although we're apart, don't block me out
I won't let you down, there is no doubt.

WE TRIED

Well here we are again
We're closer to the end
There's no need to try and save it
There's no need for us to pretend.

We tried to make it last
But still it ended fast
The only thing left for us to to do
Is let it all be in the past.

We tried to take it slow
But still we let it go
There's no way that we can stay together
Although we love each other so

Now I'm at my lowest point
I'm as far down as I can go
I refuse to try and get up again
From now on I'll just lay low.

This way no one can hurt me
And no one can play with my heart
This way I won't discover another end
Because there won't be another start.

JUST TELL ME

If you need some time to get away
Just tell me and I will make your day
If you feel you want to be alone
Just tell me so I won't keep holding on
If you think you need to think things out
Just tell me so I won't be in doubt
If you think I'm not the one for you
Just tell me so I'll know what to do
If you think you're in love with someone else
Just tell me so I'll stop torturing myself
If you think that I am wasting my time
Just tell me please and stop playing with my mind.

FORGIVE ME PLEASE

You broke up with your girl
I know how you must feel
You want me to help you work things out
But I just happen to love you still
If I tell her that you are made for each other
I'd be telling her a lie
Because if there's any two people that belong together
I think it's you and I
I cannot help you to love another
When I want you to love me
I will not tell her to come back to you
Because that not how I think it should be
I hope you will forgive me
And understand me too
Because no matter how hard I try
I can't stop love you.

DON'T LOVE ME

You looked me in the eye
I smiled and turned away
And now you wonder why
I did not want to stay.

You grabbed me by my hand
You would not let me go
You say you don't understand
Why I can't let my feeling show.

You follow me around
You seem so sure of yourself
I'm not trying to you down
But you should go find someone else.

I wish that I could tell you
Without making you feel so low
There's nothing that I can do for you
Because there are no feeling to show.

I want us to be friends
Like we were at the very start
You can trust me with your secrets
But don't trust me with your heart.

HURTS LESS TO WALK AWAY

If I walk away, it may sting for a while and then the healing begins.

If I stay, it will sting over and over as you keep doing the same heartless things.

I may as well just hurt one time as I get over you and discover a healthier me.

You can keep the stings for the next victim.

GOOD-BYE

Ever since I met you
My life has gone down stream
You've made dirt roads from my mountains
And nightmares from my dreams.
My beautiful days turn rotten
Whenever you come around
And my bright and beautiful smile
Turns quickly upside down.
I feel like I get sick
Whenever you appear
And I lose my concentration
Whenever you are near.
You've got me living in misery
And I can't let this madness go on
So take my advice while I'm nice about it
And LEAVE ME THE #*@% ALONE.

ACCUSATIONS

If I were to see your life through a crystal ball,
Would I be disappointed in you because I was right
Or would I be disappointed in myself because I was wrong?

ADDICTION

You shouldn't offer someone suffering from
drug addiction CRACK

You shouldn't offer someone suffering from
alcohol abuse DRINKS

And you shouldn't offer someone suffering from
trust issues LIES
Especially when you're the reason for the trust issues.

ALWAYS

Whatever she is telling you
To convince you that she's true
She'll never have it in her heart
To love you like I do.

Whatever he is telling me
To win my trust from me
He'll never come as close to my heart
As you will always be.

If I ever grow back my wings of love
And again learn how to fly
I'll never forget what you meant to me
And I'll never soar as high.

CHOOSE YOU

When loving him means losing yourself,
It's time to let him go.

LIVING IN THE PAST

I'm not living in the past,

I've simply learned your pattern and I know what to expect.

SHATTERED GLASS

Like shattered glass,
Some hearts are broken beyond repair.

PIECES TO A PUZZLE

Forced love doesn't fit too well. If you have to force someone
To love you or be loyal to you
It's probably best to just let it go because it will
never be a perfect fit.

TRY AGAIN

Every time you try but fail
You're one step closer to succeeding.
Keep trying.

THE STORM

He is the calm before the storm

I AM the storm.

A PLAN

A plan with no action is just a thought blowing in the wind.

WHO AM I?

Tossing and bouncing as the wind blows. The wind changes direction and I'm suddenly blown to an unknown road. I'm kicked and thrown around, sometimes so hard that the wind is knocked out of me. I'm down for a minute, unable to roll like a flat tire sitting in a puddle. Someone finds me, pumps air in me, makes me brand new again. Only to toss me back in the wind and go through the same thing again.
Who am I?
A beach ball? No!
I am love!!

FRIENDS LOVERS STRANGERS

Friends lovers or strangers
Which one will we be
Which do you find in your heart
Which do you consider me
Will we ever pick up the pieces
Will we gather what was left
Will we follow the road to a bridge
Or will I take the dirt road by myself
Friends lovers or strangers
Which one will we be?

VICTIM TO YOURSELF

The worse jail sentence is to be prisoner to yourself.

Don't be your own victim.

COURT OF LOVE

I was turned into this court
Because of my love for you
They had the evidence to prove
That without you I wouldn't know what to do
I swore to tell the truth
But I got on the stand and lied
The jury said it was clear to see
That I had lots of feeling to hide.
They asked me if I would ever in the future
Consider being your wife
And once again I told another lie
And they sentenced me to life
So there I was in the electric chair
There was nothing else to do
The judge had finally come to a decision
I was guilty of still loving you!

SUNSHINE IN THE STORM

I have been through many storms in my life. Rain, snow and sleet. Now
there's a rainbow flowing brightly through my heart because through all this pain, I found the
love that I was searching for; Deep down in myself.

DISTANT LOVE

You said we'd be together
Forever and a day
But every time I'm near you
I feel another mile away
Your look is so much different
And your touch is not the same
I wonder if it's my imagination
Or if it's all just getting lame.
I wish that we could have things
Back like they were before
Just come back into my heart
Before I close and lock the door.

SISTERS

Having a big sister is like having a protector and a best friend all wrapped in one.

GETTING IMPATIENT

My heart is slowly breaking
And my needs are going unknown
I don't know how to handle this
It seems your desire for me is gone.

I fight to hold back my tears
Don't want you to see that I'm broken
I wait for you to open the conversation
But then those words are never spoken.

I don't know what to think anymore
I wonder if you still care
Or have you just grown too comfortable
And assume I'll always be there?

This is enough to end what we have
But still I keep holding on
I don't know how much stronger I can be
Before you force my love to be gone.

CAN WE

Can we put our pride aside
Can we somehow reconcile
Can we both come to our senses
Can we sit and talk awhile
Can we figure out what's wrong
Can we put us back together
Can we continue with our lives
Can we stay in love forever?

FINDING HOPE

You lost hope?
Ok.
Now find it again. Dig deep inside.
I promise; it's there.

LOVE IS REAL

I built a wall to guard my heart
It was tall and all around
As soon as you came into my life
My walls came tumbling down.

The more I ignored your offer of love
The louder you gave to me
The more I turned the other way
The more you made me see.

You convinced me to put my trust in you
And that together we would win
I took a chance, looked in your eyes
And suddenly, I gave in.

My black and white world then came to life
My rainbow big and bright
With all the darkness that surrounded me
You made a streak of light.

You proved to me that you were true
You proved how you really feel
You showed me how you could love me right
You proved that love is real.

FAMILIAR STRANGERS

One minute we're almost strangers
The next we're sharing our thoughts
We went from zero to one hundred
Our hidden feelings suddenly caught.

Now we're spinning our wheels
Because we don't know what to do
We admitted too much to ourselves
No longer hiding what was true.

Two people who silently bonded
The real reason not being known
Two people who always connected
And now the cards are finally shown.

So where do we go from here
Do we walk away or follow our hearts
What do we do with this bond
Let it grow or tear it apart?

MAYBE NEXT LIFETIME

I only want the best for you
Even if that isn't me
I truly want you in my life
But I care enough to set you free

I don't think that you truly understand
How much I care for you
You make me feel complete
You help me to know that love is true

I can't offer you what you deserve
Because of my situation
If I had a way to make you mine
I would do it without hesitation

You deserve to find your Queen
Just let this go while you search for love
You're the one who will always have my heart
The one that I'll always be thinking of.

TO THE FELLAS

A woman doesn't fall out of love overnight.
When she's complaining crying and begging you to change
She's in the process of working on the relationship.
When you ignore her cries, she eventually starts working on her healing.
When she stops crying and complaining, she's over you.
When she walks away, you lost.
You will never get her back.
Listen to your woman's cries or you will lose her forever.

You're welcome.

MOMMA USED TO SAY

The next few pages are some quotes that
momma used to say and some scenarios where she
would use them. Momma was a wise lady
who kept her cool under any type of pressure.
Momma was also a poet and the skills that she equipped
me with made it possible to write this book. Momma is resting
in Heaven and I know she is so proud that I finally shared some
of
my work with the world.
Thank you momma for your support and patience as you stood
beside myself, my sister, my 3 children, and my nephew.
Your spirit lives through us every day and we will always live
by
the words that you taught us.

MOMMA USED TO SAY

Don't leave the house in ragged socks and underwear.
You never know what might happen.

MOMMA USED TO SAY

Always be kind to people.
One day your life may rely on someone being kind to you.

MOMMA USED TO SAY

When my sister and I used fight, momma would fuss and
Say, "Ya'll act like you don't have the same blood.
Better quit all
that fighting because

All you have is each other".

MOMMA USED TO SAY

Don't fix your husbands food on a paper plate.

MOMMA USED TO SAY

When you're having a bad day, dress up
and put on make-up. It'll make you feel better.

MOMMA USED TO SAY

You can't change stupid

MOMMA USED TO SAY

"Let's Dance"

If we were feeling down, mom would grab us
by the hand, swirl us around and
dance with us until the tears
turned into laughter.

MOMMA USED TO SAY

Never complain when someone is singing.
It's a sign that they are happy.

MOMMA USED TO SAY

Don't go to bed mad. You might not wake up.

MOMMA USED TO SAY

Don't kick a man when he's down

MOMMA USED TO SAY

Don't judge a person by their attitude. You never know what someone is going through.

MOMMA USED TO SAY

Don't be an educated fool

MOMMA USED TO SAY

Eat your vegetables. I'll sit with you.

MOMMA USED TO SAY

When you're hanging out with your friends, imagine that the stranger standing next to you is a Preacher.

MOMMA USED TO SAY

Always do your part.

MOMMA USED TO SAY

Life doesn't have to be complicated.

www.ingramcontent.com/pod-product-compliance
Lightning Source LLC
Chambersburg PA
CBHW031404040426
42444CB00005B/416